Mason Moose Meditates

Published by

INK Bubbles PUBLISHING

Port Elgin, Ontario,

Canada

2023

ISBN 978-1-7770829-9-4

Mason Moose Meditates

Mason Moose Meditates

Meditation steps

1. Put on some soft meditation music or you can have it quiet in the room.

2. Find a quiet, cozy spot

3. You can sit cross legged with your back straight or lie down

4. Place your hands on your knees facing up if you are sitting up, or, put your hands beside you, facing up if you are lying down.

5. Next you gently close your eyes

6. Focus on your breathing slowly breathe in through your nose, then slowly breathe out through your nose

7. Continue to focus on your breathing slowly breathing in and then slowly breathing out.

Mason Moose can
meditate

in his house

Slowly breathe in
and
slowly breathe out

Mason Moose can meditate

in the grass

Slowly breathe in
and
slowly breathe out

Mason Moose can meditate

at the beach

Slowly breathe in and
slowly breathe out

Mason Moose can meditate

under the sun

Slowly breathe in and
slowly breathe out

Mason Moose can meditate

at the playground

Slowly breathe in and
slowly breathe out

Mason Moose can meditate

at the campsite

Slowly breathe in and
slowly breathe out

Mason Moose can meditate

in the forest

Slowly breathe in and
slowly breathe out

Mason Moose can meditate

with friends
like you

Slowly breathe in
and
slowly breathe out

Thank you for purchasing this book.

Follow Me on Instagram @Jewel Star Writer

Look for my other Children's Picture Books,

YA Books, Planners, Journals, Educational Books,

Coloring Books, and other genres.

Published by INK Bubbles Publishing

2023